SUBLIMINAL READING

C. J. Mozzochi, Ph.D.

Note for Librarians: a cataloguing record for this book that includes Dewey Decimal Classification and US Library of Congress numbers is available from the Library and Archives of Canada. The complete cataloguing record can be obtained from their online database at:
www.collectionscanada.ca/amicus/index-e.html
ISBN 1-4120-4468-5

The ideas, suggestions and procedures contained in this book are not intended as a substitute for consulting with a therapist. In particular, before using any hypnosis techniques one should obtain a professional evaluation to determine one's suitability for using such techniques. The author and the publisher assume no responsibility for the use of the techniques described in this book.

TRAFFORD

Offices in Canada, USA, Ireland, UK and Spain

This book was published *on-demand* in cooperation with Trafford Publishing. On-demand publishing is a unique process and service of making a book available for retail sale to the public taking advantage of on-demand manufacturing and Internet marketing. On-demand publishing includes promotions, retail sales, manufacturing, order fulfilment, accounting and collecting royalties on behalf of the author.

Book sales for North America and international:
Trafford Publishing, 6E–2333 Government St.,
Victoria, BC V8T 4P4 CANADA
phone 250 383 6864 (toll-free 1 888 232 4444)
fax 250 383 6804; email to orders@trafford.com

Book sales in Europe:
Trafford Publishing (UK) Ltd., Enterprise House, Wistaston Road Business Centre,
Wistaston Road, Crewe, Cheshire CW2 7RP UNITED KINGDOM
phone 01270 251 396 (local rate 0845 230 9601)
facsimile 01270 254 983; orders.uk@trafford.com

Order online at:
www.trafford.com/robots/04-2276.html

10 9 8 7 6 5 4

Dedicated to the memory of my father and mother

Contents

Part I Reading

Preface

Chapter 1. Preview 5

Chapter 2. Subliminal Reading 7

Chapter 3. Conscious Reading 9

Chapter 4. Retention 11

Part II Self-Control

Preface

Chapter 5. The Conditioning Tape 17

Chapter 6. The Intensifying Tape 27

Chapter 7. The Releasing Tape 29

Chapter 8. The Acceptance Tape 31

Chapter 9. The Coordination Tape 33

Chapter 10. The Dream Tape 35

Chapter 11. The Dream Retrieval Tape 37

Chapter 12. The Sleep Learning Tape 39

Epilogue 41

References 43

Part I

Reading

Preface

Although hypnosis techniques for accelerating the learning process and subliminal techniques for accelerating the reading process are well known, a careful search of the literature seems to indicate that the idea of combining subliminal techniques with my so-called "direct command technique" to accelerate the reading process is original with me and consistent with the conclusions of other researchers.

Do not study Part I until you have conditioned yourself sufficiently with the conditioning tape so that you can successfully perform Experiment A and Experiment B in Part II.

C. J. Mozzochi, Ph.D.
New York City
August, 2004

Chapter 1

Preview

Sit comfortably in a well lighted area. Get completely relaxed by using the direct command technique as explained in Experiment B in Part II. Use the Temperature-Tension Colorimeter to assure that you have achieved the maximum state of relaxation.

Take possession of the book and carefully read the descriptive material and reviews on the back of the book and on the book jacket, if there is one. Read the Table of Contents, the Preface, and the Introduction, if there is one. Review the Index, and the Glossary, if there is one. Also, go through the book and examine preliminarily, but not in detail, all of the charts, graphs and tables. Briefly review all photographs and their captions.

Become familiar with the book.

Then formulate specific questions that you want answered by reading the book. Determine what information you would like to retrieve from the book. For best results, write all of this material on paper.

Chapter 2

Subliminal Reading

After completing your preview of the book read to yourself (or, for a better effect, write) five times the following statement:

> I now subliminally read this book.
> I focus both eyes on each individual page,
> as I turn the pages in sequence, in such a way
> that my eyes cover the entire page.
> I make no effort whatsoever to read words
> or sentences on any page.
> I remain totally relaxed and deep in
> hypnosis during the entire time I am
> subliminally reading this book.

Then close your eyes and command yourself to go into hypnosis as described in Experiment A in Part II. Relax all the numbers between one and one-hundred completely out of your mind. Then slowly ride an imaginary elevator, first down to Level A, then down to Level B and then down to Level C. The elevator is specal in that each time you arrive at each level you double your mental relaxation. Then, remaining in hypnosis, visualize (or think of) yourself doing exactly as specified in the above-displayed statement.

After visualizing for one to three minutes remain in hypnosis, but open your eyes.

Then read the book as described in the above-displayed statement saying to yourself as you turn each page, "stay in hypnosis." If you used the Conditioning Tape properly as instructed in Part II, then you will remain in hypnosis as you subliminally read the book. Spend one to three seconds on each page.

Keep all of the numbers between one and one-hundred completely out of your conscious mind during the entire time you are subliminally reading the book. When you are finished, command yourself to go out of hypnosis.

The playing of the slow movements in works from the baroque, classical, romantic and impressionistic and twentieth century musical periods, especially those in the works of Bach, Mozart, Beethoven, Mendelssoln and Warlock, will contribute to maintaining the hypnotic state, when reading subliminally.

Chapter 3

Conscious Reading

Sit comfortably in a well lighted area. Get completely relaxed by using the direct command technique as explained in Experiment B in Part II. Use the Temperature-Tension Colorimeter to assure that you have achieved the maximum state of relaxation.

Review your reasons for reading the book.

Then go through the book. If you have subliminally read the book properly, the sections of the book that are of interest to you should be easy to determine. Read these sections carefully at a speed that is comfortable for you to extract the information, for which you are looking.

Chapter 4

Retention

Sit comfortably in a well lighted area. Get completely relaxed by using the direct command technique as explained in Experiment B in Part II. Use the Temperature-Tension Colorimeter to assure that you have achieved the maximum state of relaxation.

If there are particular sections of a book you would like to especially retain, the following procedure due to Harry Arons is very effective. He called it the "Sandwich Method" of learning.

First you prepare two suggestion cards. Number one card No. 1 and the other No. 2. On Card No. 1 write or print the following suggestion:

"The material I am about to study will become *deeply impressed* and will be *permanently retained.*"

On Card No. 2 write or print this suggestion:

"The material that I have just learned is *permanently retained* and will be *easily recalled* when I need it."

When you prepare to study, sit at your desk or other customary place; get the material all ready before you. Then take Card No. 1, read it five times, drop it and go into hypnosis and let the suggestion simmer in your mind for the three minute period. Then come out of hypnosis and study the material for ten minutes. At the end of the ten minutes take Card no. 2, read that five times, drop it, go into hypnosis and let that suggestion simmer for three minutes. Then come out of hypnosis and spend about five minutes either watching television or reading somethng for enjoyment only. This is a rest period.

Then you take Card No. 1 and repeat the entire process. In other words, you study for ten mintues at a time with three minute hypnotic periods before and after the study period and then a five minute rest period to boot.

It can be seen from the above that by using this method only about half an hour is spent in actual studying with the rest of the time being devoted to self-hypnosis and rest. As you gain facility in the use of this method, you can extend the study period to fifteen minutes of time and possibly even eliminate the five minute rest period completely. The important thing here is that you are studying during the time when your mind is at its most alert and efficient state–before it becomes fatigued from studying.

The method gains its name from the fact that a study period is sandwiched in between two self-hypnosis periods.

It should be noted that the suggestion on Card No. 1 embodies improvement in impression and in retention, while the suggestion on Card No. 2 embodies suggestions of improvement for retention and recall. Thus the two hypnotic periods overlap on retention. Since the studying is done during the waking state, the critical faculties of the conscious mind are at their best, with post-hypnotic suggestion and self-hypnosis stimulating the subconscious mind to the improvement desired. This method can, of course, be varied in a number of ways providing the main principles are retained.

Part II

Self-Control

Preface

The purpose of this part of the monograph is to outline an extremely effective procedure for obtaining self-control through the use of tape recordings which you can easily make yourself.

Although the idea of giving commands to oneself directly without the formal use of hypnosis goes back at least to Coué (c. 1920), and no doubt much farther, a careful search of the literature seems to indicate that the idea of programming (by means of the repeated use of a recording) the subconscious mind to respond directly to arbitrary commands from the conscious mind is original with me and consistent with the conclusions of other researchers. My method helps a person to realize his or her potential in what appears to be an innate ability.

Chapter 5

The Conditioning Tape

Introduction

The purpose of the conditioning tape is to program, by means of hypnosis, your subconscious mind to accept commands directly from your conscious mind.

More specifically, the suggestion that is given to you repeatedly while you are in hypnosis is: "Whenever you want to command yourself to do something, all that you have to do is slowly repeat the command to yourself mentally. Each time you repeat the command to yourself mentally, your body and mind respond to your command with greater and greater intensity."

Once this programming is accomplished, the applications are almost unlimited.

Technical Description

The tape recording is 45 minutes long, and it starts with one minute of nothing but a forty cycle per minute beat (which occurs during the entire time the tape is playing) of an electronic metronone. The frequency of the metronone is not critical, but it should be close to this frequency.

Text

Now take a deep breath. Hold it. Exhale and relax. Now take another deep breath. Hold it. Exhale and relax. Now take a third deep breath. Hold it. Exhale and relax. Now close your eyes and relax the muscles and nerves around your eyes to the point where you feel that your eyelids simply will not work; even if you wanted them to. Now feel the relaxation building up around your eyes and send this feeling of relaxation all through your body ... into your forehead ... into your scalp ... down into your face and jaw ... down your neck ... into your shoulders ... down your arms ... into your wrists ... into your hands and into your fingers. Now send this feeling of relaxation all the way down your spine ... into your chest ... into the stomach region ... into the pelvic region ... into your hips ... into your thighs ... into your knees ... down your legs ... into your ankles ... into the arches of your feet ... into the balls of your feet and into your toes. Now when I tell you to, but not yet, I want you to open your eyes, close your eyes, and we will go through the same procedure all over again. And when you do, you will become five times as relaxed as you are now. Now open your eyes, close your eyes and relax the muscles and nerves around your eyes to the point where you feel that your eyelids simply will not work; even if your wanted them to. Now feel the relaxation building up around your eyes and send this feeling of relaxation all through your body ... into your forehead ... into your scalp ... down into your face and jaw ... down your neck ... into your shoulders ... down your arms ... into your wrists ... into your hands and into your fingers. Now send this feeling of relaxation all the way down your spine ... into your chest ... into the stomach region ... into the pelvic region ... into your hips ... into your thighs ... into your knees ... down your legs ... into your ankles ... into the arches of your feet ... into the balls of your feet and into your toes. Now when I tell you to, but not yet, I want you to open your eyes, close your eyes, and we will go through the same procedure all over again. And when we do, you will become five times as relaxed as you are now. Now open your eyes, close your eyes and relax the muscles and nerves around your eyes to the point where you feel that your eyelids simply will not work; even if you wanted them to. Now feel the relaxation building up around your eyes and send this feeling of relaxation all through your body ... into your forehead ... into your scalp ... down into your face and jaw ... down your neck ... into your shoulders ... down your arms ... into your wrists ... into your hands and into your fingers. Now send this feeling of relaxation all the way down your spine ... into your chest ... into the stomach region ... into the pelvic region ... into your hips ... into your thighs ... into your knees ... down your legs ... into your ankles ... into the arches of your feet ... into the balls of your feet and into your toes. (Pause) You are now in hypnosis. if at any time you want to return to your normal state of consciousness, just mentally count upward from one to five and say the words "fully aware." (Pause) Every time you go into hypnosis your body and mind achieve a state of profound physical, mental and emotional relaxation more easily and with greater and greater intensity. (Pause) To achieve a deeper state of physical relaxation, send a wave of relaxation from the top of your head all the way down to your toes. Imagine and feel this relaxation flowing all through your body. To achieve a deeper state of mental and emotional relaxation, relax all the thoughts and cares and worries and concerns completely out of your mind. Just become all mind and no body; and as you do, achieve a deeper state of physical, mental and emotional relaxation. Just let go and relax. To achieve a deeper state of physical relaxation send a wave of relaxation from the top of your head all the way down to your toes. Imagine and feel this relaxation flowing all through your body. To achieve a deeper state of mental and emotional relaxation, relax all the thoughts and cares and worries and concerns completely out of your mind. Just become all mind and no body; and as you do, achieve a deeper state of physical, mental and emotional relaxation. Just let go and relax. To achieve a deeper state of physical relaxation, send a wave of relaxation from the top of your head all the way down to your toes. Imagine and feel this relaxation flowing all through your body. To achieve a deeper state of mental and emotional relaxation, relax all the thoughts and cares and worries and concerns completely out of your mind. Just become all mind and no body; and as you do, achieve a deeper state of physical, mental and emotional relaxation. Just let go and relax. To achieve a deeper state of physical relaxation, send a wave of relaxation from the top of your head all the way down to your toes. Imagine and feel this relaxation flowing all through your body. To achieve a deeper state of mental and emotional relaxation, relax all the thoughts and cares and worries and concerns completely out of your mind. Just become all mind and no body; and as you do, achieve a deeper state of physical, mental and emotional relaxation. Just let go and relax. To achieve a deeper state of physical relaxation, send a wave of relaxation from the top of your head all the way down to your toes. Imagine and feel this relaxation flowing all through your body. To achieve a deeper state of mental and emotional relaxation, relax all the thoughts and cares and worries and concerns completely out of your mind. Just become all mind and no body; and as you do, achieve a deeper state of physical, mental and emotional relaxation. Just let go and relax. To achieve a deeper state of physical relaxation, send a wave of relaxation from the top of your head all the way down to your toes. Imagine and feel this relaxation flowing all through your body. To achieve a deeper state of mental and emotional relaxation, relax all the thoughts and cares and worries and concerns completely out of your mind. Just become all mind and no body; and as you do, achieve a deeper state of physical, mental and emotional relaxation. Just let go and relax. To achieve a deeper state of physical relaxation, send a wave of relaxation from the top of your head all the way down to your toes. Imagine and feel this relaxation flowing all through your body. To achieve a deeper state of mental and emotional relaxation, relax all the thoughts and cares and worries and concerns completely out of your mind. Just become all mind and no body; and as you do, achieve a deeper state of physical, mental and emotional relaxation. Just let go and relax. (Pause) Every time you go into hypnosis your body and mind achieve a state of profound physical, mental and emotional relaxation more easily and with greater and greater intensity. (Pause) Whenever you want to command yourself to do something, all that you have to do is slowly repeat the command to yourself mentally. Each time you repeat the command to yourself mentally, your body and mind respond to your command with greater and greater intensity. Whenever you want to command yourself to do something, all that you have to do is slowly repeat the command to yourself mentally. Each time you repeat the command to yourself mentally, your body and mind respond to your command with greater and greater intensity. Whenever you want to command yourself to do something, all that you have to do is slowly repeat the command to yourself mentally. Each time you repeat the command to yourself mentally, your body and mind respond to your command with greater and greater intensity. Whenever you want to command yourself to do something, all that you have to do is slowly repeat the command to yourself mentally. Each time you repeat the command to yourself mentally, your body and mind respond to your command with greater and greater intensity. Whenever you want to command yourself to do something, all that you have to do is slowly repeat the command to yourself mentally. Each time you repeat the command to yourself mentally, your body and mind respond to your command with greater and greater intensity. Whenever you want to command yourself to do something, all that you have to do is slowly repeat the command to yourself mentally. Each time you repeat the command to yourself mentally, your body and mind respond to your command with greater and greater intensity. Whenever you want to command yourself to do something, all that you have to do is slowly repeat the command to yourself mentally. Each time you repeat the command to yourself mentally, your body and mind respond to your command with greater and greater intensity. Whenever you want to command yourself to do something, all that you have to do is slowly repeat the command to yourself mentally. Each time you repeat the command to yourself mentally, your body and mind respond to your command with greater and greater intensity. Whenever you want to command yourself to do something, all that you have to do is slowly repeat the command to yourself mentally. Each time you repeat the command to yourself mentally, your body and mind respond to your command with greater and greater intensity. Whenever you want to command yourself to do something, all that you have to do is slowly repeat the command to yourself mentally. Each time you repeat the command to yourself mentally, your body and mind respond to your command with greater and greater intensity. Whenever you want to command yourself to do something, all that you have to do is slowly repeat the command to yourself mentally. Each time you repeat the command to yourself mentally, your body and mind respond to your command with greater and greater intensity. Whenever you want to command yourself to do something, all that you have to do is slowly repeat the command to yourself mentally. Each time you repeat the command to yourself mentally, your body and mind respond to your command with greater and greater intensity. Whenever you want to command yourself to do something, all that you have to do is slowly repeat the command to yourself mentally. Each time you repeat the command to yourself mentally, your body and mind respond to your command with greater and greater intensity. Whenever you want to command yourself to do something, all that you have to do is slowly repeat the command to yourself mentally. Each time you repeat the command to yourself mentally, your body and mind respond to your command with greater and greater intensity. Whenever you want to command yourself to do something, all that you have to do is slowly repeat the command to yourself mentally. Each time you repeat the commmand to yourself mentally, your body and mind respond to your command with greater and greater intensity. Whenever you want to command yourself to do something, all that you have to do is slowly repeat the command to yourself mentally. Each time you repeat the command to yourself mentally, your body and mind respond to your command with greater and greater intensity. Whenever you want to command yourself to do something, all that you have to do is slowly repeat the command to yourself mentally. Each time you repeat the command to yourself mentally, your body and mind respond to your command with greater and greater intensity. (Pause) I am now going to take you out of hypnosis and return you to your normal state of consciousness by counting upward from one to five. When I get to five, you will open your eyes. You will be completely out of hypnosis. You will be fully aware and alert and feeling good in every possible way, just as if you have had a very peaceful and relaxing night's sleep. One ... coming up slowly now ... Two ... coming up some more ... Three ... coming up some more ... Four ... almost there ... and Five ... Take a deep breath and stretch.

The Conditioning Process

In a warm and quiet room sit comfortably in a chair or recline comfortably on a bed preferably in subdued light. Be sure that you will not be disturbed by people, pets, or the telephone for at least forty-five minutes. Just relax and without effort follow the instructions that issue from the tape.

You should listen to the tape every day for one week before doing any of the experiments. You then should listen to the tape at least two or three times per week for several weeks. Then listen to the tape at least one time per week for several more weeks.

The more you listen to the tape the better will be the results that you will realize.

It is advised that you do not use any of the tapes described in this monograph immediately after you awaken from sleep, when you are very tired (except for the sleep learning tape), less than two hours after eating, or when you are driving an automobile. You will derive full benefit from these tapes even if you do not recall listening to the tape in its entirely; provided you are clearly aware of the end of the tape.

The Experiments

For best results do all of these experiments in a warm room.

A. Go Into Hypnosis

Sit down or lie down comfortably, close your eyes, and give yourself the command: "Go into hypnosis." If you have used the conditioning tape properly, you will go into hypnosis with approximately the same intensity as that obtained when you last listened to the tape.

It may be possible to reach or even exceed that intensity by repeating the above command mentally several times and/or actually saying to yourself several times mentally (or hearing): "Send a wave of relaxation from the top of your head all the way down to your toes. Relax all the thoughts and cares and worries and concerns completely out of your mind." Relax familiar things completely out of your mind such as your name and the names of people, places and things that are important to you. The more you can empty your mind, the deeper into hypnosis you will go.

Experimentation, experience, and the application to which you are applying the hypnotic state will dictate what approach you should use and when you should use it.

B. The Temperature–Tension Colorimeter

The temperature–tension colorimeter is simply a card with a plastic substance in the center which changes color according to the temperature of its surface with black indicating the low temperature end of the scale and with blue indicating the high end of the scale.

When your body is tense, the surface temperature of your skin is low; and when your body is relaxed, the surface temperature of your skin is high.

To perform the experiment simply repeat the command, "Relax," to yourself with your thumb on the plastic surface. You should with sufficient practice and repetition be able to change the color from black to blue; provided, of course, you have used the conditioning tape properly.

Since going into and staying in hypnosis is itself a relaxing process, you will be able to easily change the color of the plastic surface from black to blue by simply going into hypnosis and staying in hypnosis for a few minutes. However, there are many occasions when it would be inappropriate to go into hypnosis to relax, for example when you are in a meeting or driving your automobile.

The colorimeter is discussed in exhaustive detail in Reference [4], and it can be obtained from many sources.

C. Sound Block

Obtain a clock with an audible ticking sound. Place the clock in such a position that you are just able to hear the ticking sound. Then sit down or lie down comfortably and repeat to yourself mentally the command: "The sound of the clock is gone."

If you have used the conditioning tape properly, you will be able to block the ticking sound of the clock from your conscious mind.

D. Control of Emotions

Sit down or lie down comfortably and repeat to yourself mentally any of the commands: "Cry", "Laugh", "Be happy", "Be sad", "Be depressed", etc.

Again, if you have used the conditioning tape properly, you will be able to produce any emotion you desire to produce.

E. Pain Block

Focus your attention on the back of either your left or right hand and repeat to yourself mentally the command: "The back of my left (right) hand is completely numb and feeling good in every way."

After repeating this command for a while pinch the back of your hand very hard with the other hand. If you have conditioned yourself properly, you should not feel any pain.

Notice that if you first get very relaxed, it is easier to block the pain.

Applications

A. The Direct Command Technique

There are three ways you can use the direct command technique; after you have sufficiently conditioned yourself by listening to the conditioning tape.

1. Simply repeat the command to yourself mentally.

Example. "Go to sleep, go to sleep, go to sleep,... etc.

2. Repeat the command to yourself mentally, but add the command: "Whenever you want to command yourself to do something, all that you have to do is slowly repeat the command to yourself mentally."

Example. "Whenever you want to ..., go to sleep, go to sleep, go to sleep, go to sleep, whenever you want to ..., go to sleep, go to sleep, go to sleep, whenever you want to ..., go to sleep, go to sleep, go to sleep, go to sleep, go to sleep, ... etc."

3. First command yourself: "Go into hypnosis." Then intensify the hypnotic state as explained in Experiment A, if you so desire. Then proceed as in Method 1 or Method 2, whichever you prefer.

For some commands you may wish to first use the classical technique B below before using Method 1 or Method 2. Experimentation will allow you to decide how to proceed.

B. Classical Pre-Hypnotic Suggestion–Visualization Programming

Essentially with this technique you first consciously repeat several times a statement which states your goal. You then command yourself: "Go into hypnosis." While you are in hypnosis, you imagine and/or visualize your goal as being already achieved.

The literature on this method with its many variations and applications is extensive. The interested reader is referred to references [**1**], [**2**], [**3**], [**4**], [**5**], [**6**], [**12**], [**14**], and [**16**].

Chapter 6

The Intensifying Tape

Introduction

This tape is to be used only after one has thoroughly conditioned oneself with the conditioning tape.

The purpose of the tape is to help the user to intensify his or her hypnotic response whenever he or she goes into hypnosis with or without the tape.

The tape was developed after a year of research into the matter of the intensification of the hypnotic response.

The tape should be used once or twice per week for an indefinite period of time.

Description

The tape, which takes forty-five minutes to play, starts with one minute of nothing but a forty cycle per minute beat (which occurs during the entire time the tape is playing) of an electronic metronone. Then the following statement occurs: "Every time you go into hypnosis your body and mind achieve a state of profound physical, mental and emotional relaxation more easily and with greater and greater intensity." Then the following statement is repeated slowly for approximately forty minutes: "To achieve a deeper state of physical relaxation, send a wave of relaxation from the top of your head all the way down to your toes. Imagine and feel this relaxation flowing all through your body. To achieve a deeper state of mental and emotional relaxation, relax all the thoughts and cares and worries and concerns completely out of your mind. Just become all mind and no body; and as you do, achieve a deeper state of physical, mental, and emotional relaxation. Just let go and relax." The tape ends with a repetition of the opening statement.

The Intensifying Process

In a warm and quiet room sit comfortably in a chair or recline comfortably on a bed preferably in subdued light. Be sure that you will not be disturbed by people, pets or the telephone for at least forty-five minutes.

Start the tape and command yourself: "Go into hypnosis." Then command yourself: "Listen to and comply with the directions of the next voice that you hear." Then just relax and without effort listen to the tape. When the tape ends, you can either remain in hypnosis, or you can command yourself: "Go out of hypnosis."

Chapter 7

The Releasing Tape

Introduction

This tape is to be used only after one has thoroughly conditioned oneself with the conditioning tape.

The purpose of the tape is to release the user from unproductive thought processes.

The tape should be used once or twice per week for an indefinite period of time.

Description

The tape, which takes forty-five minutes to play, is identical for the first thirty minutes to the Intensifying Tape. Then there occurs once the following statement: "Visualize the memory portion of your mind as a vast collection of audio-visual-emotional cassette tapes. Each and every event in your life is recorded on one of these cassette tapes in vivid and perfect detail. Mentally collect in a large box all the cassette tapes in your mind that were used to record any and all unpleasant events in your life. As you mentally place each cassette in the box, mentally read the label on the cassette, which identifies the unpleasant event that it records, and mentally say to yourself: 'I forgive each person who directly or indirectly was responsible for making this event unpleasant for me, and each such person (if any exists) forgives me.' When you have finished mentally placing the cassettes in the box, mentally place this box in a very strong magnetic field, which greatly and permanently reduces the intensity of these cassettes when they are played in your mind. Then mentally remove the cassettes from the box and mentally return them to their original place in the memory portion of your mind. Each time you repeat this process the intensity of each cassettes is greatly and permanently reduced."

Use of the Tape

The tape is used in the same way as the Intensifying Tape; except that after sufficient conditioning you might want to start the tape in the middle of the first thirty minute section.

Also, it is suggested that each time before you use the tape, you make a list of the identification labels that appear on the cassettes that you intend to consider when you do use the tape.

Remain in hypnosis; as you mentally perform the operations described on the tape, after the statement has ended. Then command yourself: "Go out of hypnosis."

Chapter 8

The Acceptance Tape

Introduction

This tape is to be used only after one has thoroughly conditioned oneself with the conditioning tape.

The purpose of the tape is to help to enable a person to accept life as it is and to accept people as they are.

The tape should be used once or twice per week for an indefinite period of time.

Description

The tape, which takes forty-five minutes to play, is identical for the first thirty minutes to the Intensifying Tape. The last fifteen minutes of the tape consist of the repetition of the following statement: "Because you want to live happily and harmoniously with other people and enjoy good health, physically and emotionally, you throw a heavy yoke off your shoulders; as you forgive yourself. You forgive yourself and everybody else because you know we are all products of our inheritance and environment and that if you had been born with someone else's body, and if you had gone through the same experiences in the same order as they did, you would act exactly as they do. You accept others as they are; and when they do things you disapprove of, the only emotions you feel are sympathy and understanding. You realize a great feeling of peace and tranquillity; as you forgive yourself and start with a clean slate. You are in complete control of your emotions at all times, even under what others believe to be stressful conditions. You accept life as it is, and you accept people as they are. You are relaxed and controlled, and your bodily functions are working perfectly as a result. You accept the world as it is, and you go along with the tide. As you relax and accept life, your health improves daily, and you feel great. You feel happier every day, healthier every day. You enjoy life, and you enjoy people. You are constantly growing and maturing and realizing a new sense of self-confidence. You are aware of a new freedom. Your judgment is good, and you are fully capable of making the proper decisions."

Use of the Tape

The tape is used in the same way as the Intensifying Tape; except that after sufficient conditioning you might want to start the tape in the middle of the first thirty minute section.

Chapter 9

The Coordination Tape

Introduction

This tape is to be used only after one has thoroughly conditioned oneself with the conditioning tape.

The purpose of the tape is to coordinate the user's conscious mind and subconscious mind; so that he or she will be able to study, work and create with optimum efficiency.,

The tape should be used once or twice per week for an indefinite period of time.

Description

The tape, which takes forty-five minutes to play, is identical for the first twenty five minutes to the Intensifying Tape. The last twenty minutes of the tape consist of the repetition of the following statement: "Every time you study, read, work or attend a lecture you find it easier and easier to concentrate. You are and you remain very physically, mentally and emotionally relaxed, and your mind is extremely alert. you disregard all distractions that are not an emergency. Your powers of concentration, and your attention span are tremendously increased. Your concentration is perfect. You understand ideas and concepts the first time you encounter them. Your mind works faster and faster. Time seems to pass slower and slower; as your mind works faster and faster. The material that you study is firmly impressed on your mind and permanently retained in your subconscious mind. This material is automatically subconsciously coded; so that it can be recalled easily at any time. Your conscious mind and your subconscious mind work together in balanced harmony, rapidly exchanging information with each other. When you work to solve a problem, any information that is stored in your subconscious mind that relates to a solution of the problem, is easily recalled. You are a very creative person. All of your ideas are novel and useful. Your mind is very flexible when you are solving problems; and new ideas and new approaches to problems come easily to you. You realize and truly believe that nobody is any smarter or has more mental ability than you do. Anything that any other human being can do with regard to learning, recalling, and creating you can do also."

Use of the Tape

The tape is used in the same way as the Intensifying Tape; except that after sufficient conditioning you might want to start the tape in the middle of the first twenty-five minute section.

Chapter 10

The Dream Tape

Introduction

This tape is to be used only after one has thoroughly conditioned oneself with the conditioning tape.

The purpose of the tape is to help the user to dream and to utilize sleep time in a more systematic and useful way.

The tape should be used once or twice per week for an indefinite period of time.

Description

The tape, which takes forty-five minutes to play, is identical for the first thirty minutes to the Intensifying Tape. The last fifteen minutes of the tape consist of the repetition of the following statement: "When sleeping you always dream and think subconsciously without disturbing the recuperative value of your natural sleep. You always consciously remember in vivid and accurate detail your dreams and subconscious insights, when you awaken. The very first thing you do when you awaken is consciously review the dreams and subconscious insights that occurred during the previous period of sleep. You always dream or subconsciously think or subconsciously review in literal terms or in symbols that your conscious mind always understands. Whenever you decide to sleep, and at that time, to dream about a certain topic, or to subconsciously think about a certain problem that requires a solution, or to subconsciously think about certain material that requires review, you go into hypnosis three times: Two distinct times several hours before going to sleep, and once just before going to sleep. Each time your prehypnotic suggestion contains the dream topic, or the problem to be solved, or the material to be reviewed and the statement, 'I always consciously remember and understand my dreams and subconscious insights completely when I awaken.'"

Use of the Tape

The tape is used in the same way as the Intensifying Tape; except that after sufficient conditioning you might want to start the tape in the middle of the first thirty minute section.

Chapter 11

The Dream Retrieval Tape

Introduction

This tape is to be used with the Dream Tape.

Description

The tape, which takes six and three-quarters minutes to play, starts with the statement: "You can hear me, but you can't wake up." This statement is repeated for a total of twenty times at slowly increasing volume. Then three repetitions of the following statement occur: "In a fifteen minute time interval immediately after I stop talking, you consciously, vividly recall and review in accurate detail, and you understand completely all of the dreams and subconscious insights that have occurred during this entire present period of sleep. When the fifteen minute time interval ends, you return to your normal state of consciousness. You then are fully aware and alert, and you then immediately record these dreams and subconscious insights in your dream log." The tape ends with the statement: "I stop talking now."

Use of the Tape

Set the timer for the dream retrieval tape player for a time approximately one-half hour before you want to awaken.

Chapter 12

The Sleep Learning Tape

Introduction

The present state of research into sleep learning indicates that without using sophisticated brain wave monitoring equipment the times best suited for sleep learning are during the first one and one-half hour (approximately) immediately after you go to sleep and during the last one and one-half hour (approximately) of sleep before you awaken.

Description

The tape, which takes eight and one-half minutes to play, starts with the statement: "You can hear me, but you can't wake up." This statement is repeated for a total of twenty times at slowly increasing volume. Then three repetitions of the following statement occur: "When I stop talking, you hear a recorded voice (or voices). You allow this voice (or voices) to flow into your subconscious mind, but you do not wake up. You allow this voice (or voices) to flow into your subconscious mind, but you do not wake up. The information contained in this voice (or voices) is permanently retained in your subconscious mind, and it is automatically subconsciously coded; so that it can be recalled easily at any time. When this recorded voice (or voices) stops, you return to the sleep state you were in before I started talking to you, and you sleep deeply." The tape ends with the statement, "I stop talking now."

Use of the Tape

A separate tape player and timer are needed for the sleep learning tape. The output from this player should be used in the same amplifier which is fed by the program source.

Set the timer for the sleep learning tape player for a time approximately fifteen minutes after you go to bed or one and one-half hours (approximately) before you awaken. The timer for the program source should be set; so that the program source comes on immediately after the sleep learning tape ends. Do not make any attempt to remain awake while the program source is playing.

If you are using the first option, then during the fifteen minute time interval before the tape starts you should use the direct command technique to go into (at least) a light sleep.

It should be pointed out that each of the scripts given here for the acceptance tape, the coordination tape and the dream tape could be recorded on a repeating tape and used in conjunction with the sleep learning tape.

In fact, if one uses a continuously reversible cassette player (or players) the subliminal cassette (or cassettes) discussed in Part I, Chapter 4 can play throughout the night; however, in this mode of usage do not use the subliminal cassette (or cassettes) in conjunction with the Sleep Learning Tape, but rather allow this program source to run alone without a hypnotic-trance introduction.

Epilogue

The research of many individuals indicates that when a person uses hypnosis on a regular basis his or her body automatically tends to become self-regulating and many bad habits spontaneously disappear with or without suggestion. Use the tapes regularly, and you will reap great benefits from them.

Hypnosis is a fascinating subject, and the interested reader is urged to pursue the references given here; for I purposely restricted the scope of my text, because I felt that I could not significantly improve upon the expositions in them.

The references are directly to the layman. Persons with scientific training in psychology and/or related subjects might be interested in reading research papers in the following journals: The American Journal of Clinical Hypnosis, The International Journal of Clinical and Experimental Hypnosis, The Journal of Suggestive-Accelerative Learning and Teaching, and The Journal of Mental Imagery. Recommended also are the books: *Hypnotherapy* by David Elman, *Clinical and Experimental Hypnosis* by William S. Kroger.

References

1. Arons, H., *Hypnosis for Speeding Up the Learning Process.*
2. Arons, H., *Handbook of Self-Hypnosis.*
3. Arons, H., *How to Formulate Suggestions for Hypnosis and Self-Hypnosis.*
4. Barrios, A., Ph.D., *Toward Greater Freedom and Happiness.*
5. Bry, A. and M. Bair, *Visualization: Directing the Movies of Your Mind*, Barnes and Nobel Books, New York, 1979.
6. Burnap, R., M.D., *Reflex Conditioning.*
7. Clement, P., *Hypnosis and Power Learning.*
8. Garfield, P., Ph.D., *Creative Dreaming*, Ballantine Books, New York, 1974.
9. Gibson, H., *Hypnosis Its Nature and Therapeutic Uses*, Toplinger Publishing Co., New York, 1980.
10. Kreskin, *Kreskin's Mind Power Book*, McGraw-Hill Book Co., New York, 1977.
11. Krivy, L., Ph.D., *Learn While You Sleep.*
12. Maltz, M., Ph.D., *Psyco-Cybernetics*, Prentice-Hall, Inc., Englewood Cliffs, NJ, 1960.
13. Ostrander, S., L. Schroeder, and N. Ostrander, *Super-Learning*, Delacorte Press/Confucian Press, New York, 1979.

14. Samuels, M., M.D. and N. Samuels, *Seeing with the Mind's Eye*, Random House, Inc., New York, 1975.

15. Segall, M., *The Questions They Ask About Hypnosis.*

16. Tebbetts, C., *Self-Hypnosis and Other Mind Expanding Techniques.*

Order Form

For a free copy of the Conditioning Tape and the Temperature-Tension Colorimeter fill out this form and mail it to

C. J. Mozzochi, Ph.D.
Box 1424
Princeton, NJ 08542

Name ______________________________

Address ______________________________

____

____

____

Only this original form will be accepted. Copies will be discarded.

www.ingramcontent.com/pod-product-compliance
Ingram Content Group UK Ltd.
Pitfield, Milton Keynes, MK11 3LW, UK
UKHW041844190726
13854UKWH00002B/709

9 781412 044684